W9-BIF-331

WITHDRAWN

DECATHLON, HIGH JUMP, AND OTHER FIELD EVENTS
by Jason Page

CONTENTS

Crabtree Publishing Company
www.crabtreebooks.com

Editor: Robert Walker
Proofreader: Mike Hodge
Acknowledgements: We would like to thank Ian Hodge, Hazel Poole, Ben Hubbard and Elizabeth Wiggans for their assistance.
Cartoons by: John Alston

Picture Credits: t = top, b = bottom, l = left, r = right, OFC = outside front cover, OBC = outside back cover, IFC = front cover
All images are courtesy of Allsport, except for
AP/ PA photos: 26c. Giuliano Bevilacqua/ Rex Features: 10/11c, 20bl. Nicholas Gouhier/ABACA/PA Photos: OFC. Tony Marshall/ EMPICS Sport/ PA Photos: 22/23c, 25br. Heikki Saukkomaa/ Rex Features: 16t. Vandystadt: 12/13c
Picture research by Image Select

Library and Archives Canada Cataloguing in Publication

Page, Jason
Decathlon, high jump and other field sports / Jason Page.

(The Olympic sports)
Includes index.
ISBN 978-0-7787-4014-8 (bound).--ISBN 978-0-7787-4031-5 (pbk.)

1. Track and field--Juvenile literature. 2. Olympics--Juvenile literature.
I. Title. II. Series: Page, Jason. Olympic sports

GV1060.55.P33 2008   j796.43   C2008-900972-X

Library of Congress Cataloging-in-Publication Data

Page, Jason.
Decathlon, high jump, and other field events / Jason Page.
p. cm. -- (The Olympic sports)
Includes index.
ISBN-13: 978-0-7787-4014-8 (rlb)
ISBN-10: 0-7787-4014-5 (rlb)
ISBN-13: 978-0-7787-4031-5 (pb)
ISBN-10: 0-7787-4031-5 (pb)
1. Decathlon--Juvenile literature. 2. Olympics--Juvenile literature.
I. Title. II. Series.

GV1060.79.P34 2008
796.42--dc22

2008004907

Crabtree Publishing Company
www.crabtreebooks.com   1-800-387-7650

Published in Canada
Crabtree Publishing
616 Welland Ave.
St. Catharines, Ontario
L2M 5V6

Published in the United States
Crabtree Publishing
PMB16A
350 Fifth Ave., Suite 3308
New York, NY 10118

Published by CRABTREE PUBLISHING COMPANY Copyright © **2008**
All rights reserved. No part of this publication may be reproduced, stored in a retrieval system or be transmitted in any form or by any means, electronic, mechanical, photocopying, recording, or otherwise, without the prior written permission of Crabtree Publishing Company.
Published in the United Kingdom © 2000 by ticktock Entertainment Limited. Revised edition published in the United Kingdom © 2008 by ticktock Media Ltd. The right of the author to be identified as the author of this work has been asserted by him.

FIELD EVENTS

This book contains everything you need to know about field events and their Olympic history, plus the full lowdown on the modern pentathlon and triathlon.

TRACK & FIELD

Athletic events are grouped together in two categories. Running races are known as track events — these include sprints, hurdles, relays, medium- and long-distance races. Events that involve throwing or jumping are called field events, and it's these that we'll be looking at in detail in this book.

Field events take place in the area inside the stadium track.

Olympic Stadium, Atlanta, USA

The high jump — with a soft mat for landing!

SUPER STATS

Around four billion people worldwide are expected to watch the 2008 Beijing Olympics on television. If the entire audience held hands, they could circle Earth more than 10 times!

SOMETHING OLD, SOMETHING NEW

The modern pentathlon has its roots in the ancient Olympic Games. The triathlon, on the other hand, is a new sport. It was included for the first time at the Sydney Olympics in 2000.

RAY-MARKABLE!

Between 1900 and 1908, an American athlete named Ray Ewry won 10 gold medals in three different jumping events. That's more than anyone else has ever won in any Olympic sport!

These are the tracks for the long jump and triple jump.

The throwing circle for the discus and hammer events. A safety net protects the crowd.

OLYMPICS FACT-FILE

The Olympic Games were first held in Olympia, in ancient Greece, around 3,000 years ago. They took place every four years, until they were abolished in 393 BCE.

A Frenchman called Pierre de Coubertin (1863–1937) revived the Games, and the first modern Olympics were held in Athens in 1896.

The modern Games have been held every four years since 1896, except in 1916, 1940, and 1944, due to war. Special 10th-anniversary Games took place in 1906.

The motto of the Olympic Games is *citius, altius, fortius,* which means faster, higher, stronger in Latin.

MODERN OLYMPIANS

Jackie Joyner-Kersee (USA)

The Olympics have changed a great deal since the first modern Games were held in 1896. One of the biggest changes has been the number of female athletes taking part. Women now compete in many events that traditionally were just for men — including the pole vault, the javelin, the triathlon and the modern pentathlon!

HIGH JUMP

To stand a chance of winning a medal, Olympic high jumpers have to leap more than 7 feet (2.1m) into the air. That's like jumping over the top of your front door!

DID YOU KNOW?

High jumpers are allowed to touch the crossbar as they jump over it. However, if the bar falls down, the jump doesn't count.

In the event of a tie (when two athletes have jumped the same height), the gold medal is awarded to the one who has knocked down the crossbar the least number of times.

Dora Ratjen (GER) came in fourth in the Women's high jump in 1936. However, "Dora" was later disqualified when it was discovered that "she" was actually a man in disguise!

THREE STRIKES & YOU'RE OUT!

High jumpers are allowed only three attempts at each jump. Those who get over the crossbar without knocking it down go on to the next round of the competition; those who don't are knocked out. In each round, the bar gets at least 0.8 inches (2 cm) higher. Whoever manages to clear the highest jump wins.

SHAPE UP

Olympic athletes come in all shapes and sizes. Top high jumpers such as Charles Austin (USA), who won gold at the last Olympic Games, tend to be tall and thin with long legs.

Austin (USA)

ANIMAL OLYMPIANS

The high jump champ of the animal kingdom is a small African antelope called the "klipspringer." Springy by name and by nature, the klipspringer can leap 25 feet (7.6m) into the air — that's more than three times the human high jump record!

HAPPY LANDINGS

The rules state that high jumpers must take off from one foot, not two. To help them leap as high as possible, they are allowed to take a run-up — this can be as long or as short as they like. A soft landing bed is placed on the other side of the jump to stop them from injuring themselves when they land.

WHAT A FLOP!

In the 1968 Olympic Games, a high jumper named Dick Fosbury (USA) caused a sensation — by jumping over the bar backwards! Until Fosbury came along, high jumpers had always jumped forward, landing face down on the mat. Fosbury's revolutionary technique won him the gold medal and is now used by almost all Olympic high jumpers. It is known as the "Fosbury Flop"

MEN'S RECORDS – WORLD: Stefka Kostadinova (BUL) – 2.09 meters. **OLYMPIC**: Yelena Slesarenko (RUS) – 2.06 meters.

SAND PITS

Long jumpers land in a pit filled with soft sand. The sand helps to break their fall so that the athletes don't injure themselves. It also shows how far they jumped. Each jump is measured from the edge of the take-off board to the nearest mark made in the sand by the jumper's body.

CLOSE TO THE EDGE

Long jumpers are allowed to take a run-up, but they are not allowed to tread beyond the white take-off board. Along the edge of this board is a line of soft putty. If an athlete steps over the edge, a mark will be made in the putty, and the jump will not be counted.

DID YOU KNOW?

If the judge next to the take-off board raises a red flag it means the athlete stepped over the board and the jump has been disallowed. A white flag means the jump was OK.

The long jump was one of the original events in the ancient Olympic Games.

Unlike modern athletes, ancient Roman and Greek competitors were allowed to swing special weights made of stone or lead to help them jump farther.

OLYMPIC GOLDEN BOY

Carl Lewis (USA) is one of the greatest athletes of all time. At the 2004 Games, he won the long jump for the fourth time in a row. But that's not all. Victories in the 100m, 200m, and 400m relay have earned Lewis no less than nine golds and one silver in his Olympic medal collection.

Carl Lewis (USA)

LONG JUMP

To help them leap great distances, long jumpers need a really fast run-up. So it's not surprising that one of the greatest Olympic long jumpers is also a champion sprinter!

JUMPING INTO THE RECORD BOOKS

Long jumper Bob Beamon (USA) leapt into Olympic history during the 1968 Games in Mexico with an incredible jump measuring 29 feet (8.8m). Beamon's jump shattered the world record of over 27 (8.2m) feet held by Ralph Boston (USA) and set a new Olympic record that still stands to this day.

ANIMAL OLYMPIANS

The common flea can jump 13 inches (33 cm). That's 220 times the length of its own body. If humans could do the same, we'd be able to leap more than the length of four football fields!

WOMEN'S RECORDS – WORLD: Galina Chistyakova (URS) – 7.52 meters. **OLYMPIC:** Jackie Joyner-Kersee (USA) – 7.40 meters.

TRIPLE JUMP

The triple jump is three jumps in one. Winning gold in this event takes balance and agility, as well as power.

GOLDEN GIRL

In 1996, Inessa Kravets (UKR) became the first female triple jumper to win an Olympic gold medal. This picture was taken the year before at the World Championships where she broke the Women's world record.

ANIMAL OLYMPIANS

The gold medal in the triple jump at the animal Olympics goes to the South African sharp-nosed frog. One frog, named Santjie, managed to cover 11.26 yards (10.3m) in three leaps during a frog race in May 1977 — a record that still hasn't been broken!

Inessa Kravets (USA)

VIKTOR'S VICTORIES

The most successful Olympic triple jumper ever was Viktor Saneyev (URS). He competed in every Olympic Games from 1968 to 1980, winning three gold medals in a row, as well as a silver. (And by the looks of this photo, Saneyev could have taken the gold for "funniest jumping face.")

Viktor Saneyev (URS)

HOP, STEP & JUMP

The triple jump is similar to the long jump, but instead of one mighty leap, triple jumpers have to do three! The first is a hop (landing on the same foot that you took off from), the second is a step (landing on the other foot), and the third is a jump (landing feet-first in the sand pit).

BALANCING ACT

Watch closely and you'll notice how triple jumpers swing their arms during the final part of the jump. This helps them keep their balance as they fly through the air.

DID YOU KNOW?

The Men's triple jump has been part of the Olympic Games since 1896, but women weren't allowed to compete in the event until 1996 — 100 years later!

James Connolly (USA) became the first ever modern Olympic champion when he won the triple jump in 1896.

According to the modern rules, Connolly would have been disqualified because he took two hops and a jump rather than a hop, skip, and jump.

DID YOU KNOW?

♫ Pole vaulters can jump more than 19 feet (5.8m) into the air — that's like leaping over a giraffe!

♫ Competitors are allowed to wrap tape around the pole to add extra grip and to stop the end of the pole from getting damaged.

♫ The Olympic record for the pole vault at the first Games in 1896 was 11 feet (3.4m). It now stands at over 20 feet (6.1m)!

UP, UP, AND AWAY

Pole vaulters use a long, bendy pole to spring over enormous jumps. As they run up to the jump, they push one end of the pole into a box that's sunk into the ground just in front of the jump. This causes the pole to bend, and by hanging on to the other end, the athletes hurl themselves up into the air.

BRILLIANT BUBKA

Sergey Bubka (UKR)

Sergey Bubka (UKR) pulled off a spectacular jump in the 1988 Olympic Games. Having knocked the bar over on his two previous attempts, he managed to leap 5.9m (19.36 feet) with his last jump, breaking the Olympic record and winning the gold medal. Bubka's Olympic record was broken at the 2004 Games, but he still holds the world record with a jump of 6.14m (20.14 feet).

POLE VAULT

Women were allowed to compete in the pole vault for the first time in Olympic history at the 2000 Sydney Games. The pole vault is considered the highest and most daring Olympic event!

GOOD AS GOLD

Stacy Dragila became the first ever Women's Olympic pole vault champion in Sydney in 2000. She won gold for the USA with a clearance of over 15 feet (4.6m).

Yelena Isinbayeva (RUS)

ANIMAL OLYMPIANS

Mako sharks don't need a pole to help them jump — they've got their powerful tails! With a flick of their fins, these fearsome fish can leap more than 22 feet (6.7m) above the water. That's higher than the world record.

POLES APART

The first pole vaulters used wooden poles. Later poles were made of bamboo, which is more springy. Then, in the 1950s, aluminum poles were introduced. The latest poles are now made of fiberglass, which is light and flexible, but also very strong.

SHOT PUT

This event dates back to the ancient Olympic Games. The idea is to hurl a heavy ball as far as possible.

"PUT" IT THIS WAY

Competitors must "put" (meaning push) the shot — they are not allowed to throw it! To gain as much power as possible, they stand at the back of the throwing circle, facing the wrong way. Then, with the shot tucked against the sides of their necks, they spin around. As they do so, they straighten their arms pushing the heavy balls up into the air with an explosion of energy.

A raised "stop board" is placed along the front edge of the throwing circle. Shot-putters may touch the side of the board with their feet, but they must not step on top of it — even after the shot has landed.

ANIMAL OLYMPIANS

The shot put champion at the animal Olympics is the dung beetle. Despite their small size, these little bugs collect huge balls of elephant manure to lay their eggs in. These balls can be bigger than a shot put, but the beetles push them around with ease!

Competitors must not step outside the throwing circle until the th has been completed. The circle measures about 7 f (2.1m) across.

The shot must land tween these two white lines. it falls outside the lines, the throw doesn't count.

WEIGH TO GO

The Men's shot weighs 16 pounds (7.3 kg) and can measure up to 5 inches (12.7 cm) across — about the same size as a grapefruit, only much heavier. The shot used by women athletes is lighter and slightly smaller. It weighs in at almost 9 pounds (4.1 kg) and has a diameter of 4 inches (10.2 cm).

THE ROAD TO GOLD

The first thing you have to do if you want to win a gold medal in the shot put (or any of the other throwing events), is to qualify by throwing the minimum required distance. This gets you into the finals where you have three throws. If you end up in the top eight, you then get three more throws. And if you manage to throw farther than anyone else — you get the gold!

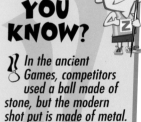

DID YOU KNOW?

In the ancient Games, competitors used a ball made of stone, but the modern shot put is made of metal.

Women competed in the shot put for the first time in 1948.

The first ever female champion was a French concert pianist called Micheline Ostermeyer, who also won gold in the discus and a bronze medal in the high jump!

DISCUS

The key to success in the discus event is a powerful but controlled throw. The launch must be smooth, for if the discus wobbles, it won't fly as far.

IN A SPIN

To launch the discus with as much power as possible, the athletes spin themselves around with their arms outstretched. Here's one-time Olympic champion Ilke Wyludda (GER) showing

DISCUS DIMENSIONS

The Men's discus measures 20 cm across and weighs 4.4 pounds (2 kg) — making it 0.79 inches (2 cm) larger and twice as heavy as the Women's discus. Athletes in ancient Greece threw a discus made of solid bronze. These days, discuses are usually made of wood with a metal rim. As you can see from this picture, the discus is much fatter in the middle than around the edge.

FANTASTIC FOUR

The greatest discus thrower the Olympics has ever seen was Al Oerter (USA). He won the gold medal four times in a row between 1956 and 1968, setting a new Olympic record each time. Only two other people have won four consecutive golds in the same event. One is the yachtsman Paul Elvstöm (DEN) in the Men's single-handed dinghy event. Do you know who the other one is? You'll find the answer on page 3.

The discus is the only throwing event in which the Women's records (both world and Olympic) are farther than the Men's records!

Ilke Wyludda (GER)

SAFETY NET

Competitors must throw the discus from a "throwing circle" — just like shot-putters. This circle is 8.2 feet (2.5m) across, making it slightly larger than the one used in other throwing events. It's surrounded on three sides by a wire cage or net, which stops the discus from being accidentally thrown toward the crowd.

DID YOU KNOW?

No man has ever broken a world record in the discus at the Olympics!

Competitors must not step outside of the throwing circle until the discus has hit the ground — if they do, the throw will be disallowed.

The ancient Greeks considered the winner of the discus to be the greatest athlete of all.

MEN'S RECORDS – WORLD: Gabriele Reinsch (GDR) – 76.80 meters. **OLYMPIC**: Martina Hellmann (GDR) – 72.30 meters.

JAVELIN

This event is a spear-throwing contest. It began as part of the military training for ancient Greek soldiers!

GET A GRIP

There are three different ways to hold a javelin. Most champions use the "Finnish" method. This involves gripping the javelin between your thumb and your last three fingers with your index finger underneath it.

YOU BE THE JUDGE

For a throw to count, the javelin must land within the fan-shaped landing area at the end of the run-up. It must also land point-first — although it doesn't have to stick in the ground.

Osleidys Menéndez (CUB)

SUPER STATS

To set a new world record in the Men's javelin, you would have to throw almost 328 feet (100m). That's more than three times the length of the longest dinosaur!

MEN'S RECORDS – WORLD: Jan Zelezny (CZE) – 90.17 meters. **OLYMPIC**: Jan Zelezny (CZE) – 90.17 meters.

FARTHER & FARTHER

Erik Lemming (SWE) won the first Olympic javelin competition in 1906 with a throw of 176.8 feet (53.9m). Over the years, the winning throw has gotten longer and longer. By 1976, the Men's Olympic record stood at 310.3 feet (94.58). Then, in 1984, Uwe Hohn (GDR) set a new world record with a throw of 343.8 (104.8).

The 2004 Women's Olympic champion is Osleidys Menéndez (CUB), seen here competing at the 2000 Games.

RECORD COLLECTION

This diagram shows how the Men's Olympic javelin record has increased since 1906.

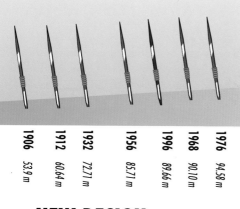

1906	1912	1932	1956	1996	1968	1976
53.9 m	60.64 m	72.71 m	85.71 m	89.66 m	90.10 m	94.58 m

NEW DESIGN

The judges feared that if throws continued to get longer, one day a javelin would land on the running track. So the design of the Men's javelin was changed, making it harder to throw. The current Men's Olympic record with the new-style javelin is 295.8 feet (90.17m) and the world record now stands at 321.5 feet (98.48m).

DID YOU KNOW?

At the ancient Olympic Games, prizes were awarded in the javelin for accuracy as well as for the greatest distance thrown.

Matti Järvinen (FIN) broke the world javelin record no fewer than 11 times between 1930 and 1936.

Javelin throwers are allowed to put resin on their hands to improve their grip, but wearing gloves is forbidden.

HAMMER TIME

The hammer doesn't actually look like a hammer at all. It's a metal ball attached to a strong metal wire with a handle on the end. The hammer weighs the same as the shot put — 16 pounds (7.26 kg) in the Men's event and 8.8 pounds (4 kg) in the new Women's event.

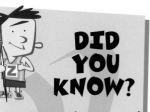

DID YOU KNOW?

Hammer throwers stand in a throwing circle 7.02 feet (2.14m) across — the same size as the circle used by shot-putters. Like discus throwers, they are surrounded by a safety net.

The USA won every single hammer competition from 1900 to 1924 — but has only won the event once since then!

Although the hammer is the same weight as the shot, it can be thrown almost four times as far!

A FEMALE FIRST

Polish athlete Kamila Skolimowska was the first woman to win a gold medal in the hammer in the 2000 Sydney Games. She beat the world champion and favorite to win Romanian Mihaela Melinte.

SUPER STATS

The hammer used in the Men's event is five times heavier than a human brain!

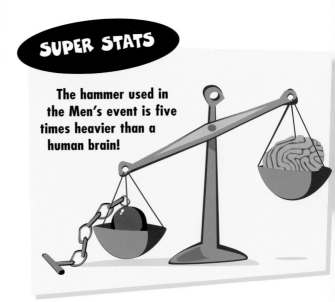

THE HAMMER

What does it take to be a champion hammer thrower? If you think that the answer is plenty of muscle and a fine sense of balance, you've hit the nail on the head!

HOW TO DO IT

Stand at the back of the circle facing the wrong way. Grip the handle with both hands, then swing the hammer around your head. When the hammer has gained enough momentum, spin yourself around the circle three or four times...then let go!

This picture shows Balazs Kiss (HUN), who won gold in the 1996 Games.

MEN'S RECORDS – WORLD: Tatyana Lysenko (RUS) – 78.67 meters. **OLYMPIC:** Olga Kuzenkova (RUS) – 75.02 meters.

THE HEPTATHLON

The heptathlon is for female competitors only, and combines seven different athletic events.

BUSY DAYS

The heptathlon is spread over two days, and the seven events are always held in the same order. Day one kicks off with the 100m hurdles. This is followed by the high jump, the shot put, then the 200m. Day two begins with the long jump. Next comes the javelin, and, last but not least, the 800m.

ANIMAL OLYMPIANS

The kangaroo would certainly be able to take the heptathlon's jumping events in its stride. These powerful animals can high jump over 9.8 feet (3m) and long jump more than 29.5 feet (9m). With a top speed of 18.6 MPH (30 km/h), the running races should be a walkover too — although the throwing events might not be so easy!

Göteborg 2006

2004 CHAMPION

Swedish athlete Carolina Klüft, seen here hur won gold in the 2004 Olympic games, and i only competitor to ever win three world titles heptathlon. She is regarded as one of the be female athletes in the world.

GET THE POINT?

Competitors are awarded points according to the distance, height, or time that they achieve in each of the events. This means that someone who performs well in all of the events but doesn't actually win any of them will probably beat someone who wins one event but does badly in all of the others. That's why it's important to be a good all-around athlete!

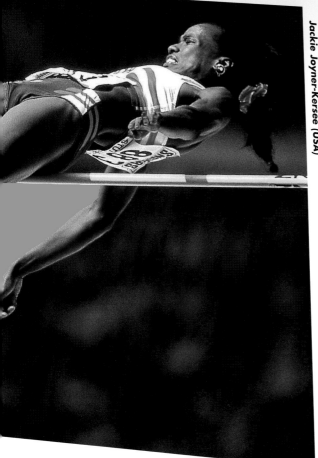

Jackie Joyner-Kersee (USA)

DID YOU KNOW?

⁇ The heptathlon was included in the Olympic Games for the first time in 1984.

⁇ In 1981, the heptathlon replaced the original pentathlon (not to be confused with the modern pentathlon) which had just five events.

⁇ Jackie Joyner-Kersee's sister-in-law was the famous sprinter Florence Griffith-Joyner, who won gold medals in the 100m 200m and 4x100m relay.

JUMPING FOR JOY-NER

Jackie Joyner-Kersee (USA) missed the gold medal by just five points at the 1984 Games. However, in 1988, she made certain of the gold — smashing her own world record by 76 points! In 1992, she won the heptathlon for a second time and has also won one gold and two bronze medals in the long jump.

SHOE BUSINESS

Decathletes need at least five different pairs of shoes! A running shoe (with short spikes), a long jump shoe (with longer spikes), a high jump shoe (spikes on the heel as well as the toe) a discus/shot put shoe (no spikes) and a javelin shoe (spikes and support around the ankle).

DID YOU KNOW?

♫ The very first Olympic decathlon held in 1904 was quite different from the modern competition today. Events included throwing a 56 pound (25.55 kg) weight and an 880 yard (805m) walk!

♫ In 1912, the decathlon was won by Jim Thorpe (USA), who went on to become one of America's greatest ever football and baseball stars.

♫ Thorpe was later disqualified (on the grounds that he was a professional athlete) but in 1982, 29 years after his death, the International Olympic Committee changed its mind and reinstated him.

THE DALEY NEWS

The first ever decathlon was won by an athlete named Thomas Kiely (GBR) in 1904. However, Britain didn't win another medal in the event until 1980, when Daley Thompson won the gold. This picture of Thompson was taken on his way to a second victory at the next Olympics in 1984.

THE DECATHLON

The decathlon is like the heptathlon, except that this competition is for men only and is made up of 10 different disciplines.

O'BRIEN vs CZECH REPUBLIC

Dan O'Brien (USA) broke the world record in 1992 and won the gold in 1996. However, his record was broken by Tomas Dvorak (CZE) in 1997 and then by Roman Sebrle (CZE) in 2004. Roman Sebrle, pictured on the left, currently holds both the Olympic and World records.

KEEP GOING

Stamina is the key to success in the decathlon. Competitors take part in 10 events in just two days — three jumps, three throws, and four races. On the first day, they tackle the 100m, long jump, shot put, high jump, and 400m, in that order. On the second day, they compete in the 110m hurdles, discus, pole vault, javelin, and 1500m. Phew!

Decathletes need to be fast as well as strong. But even they can't sprint as quickly as a pet cat! The fastest a human can run is around 21.4 MPH (35 km/h), but cats have a top speed of almost 31.1 MPH (50 km/h).

ANIMAL OLYMPIANS

THE TRIATHLON

The Triathlon is a relatively new Olympic sport, which made its first appearance at the Sydney Games.

SPLASH, PEDAL, SPRINT

The triathlon is a gruelling, non-stop race that combines swimming, cycling, and running. The 50 athletes who start each race begin by swimming 1.5 km, then (without taking a rest) they have to jump on a bicycle and cycle another 40 km. But the end of the bike ride isn't the end of the race — they then have to run another 10 km on foot to get to the finish line!

Special triathlon handle bars called "tri-bars" allow the cyclist to crouch very low, reducing wind resistance and allowing the bike to go faster.

ANIMAL OLYMPIANS

The Olympic triathlon course covers 32 miles (51.5 km) in total. It would take the average tortoise about 140 hours to travel this far. Human competitors usually complete the course in around two hours!

The cycles used in the triathlon are lightweight racing bikes.

ULTRA TOUGH

Triathlon courses can be different lengths. The toughest is known as the "ultra course." This involves a 2.36 mile (3.8 km) swim, a 111.8 mile (180 km) cycle ride (often through the mountains) and a 26 mile (42 km) run. The best competitors can finish it in about 8 hours!

All competitors must wear helmets during the bike race.

Loretta Harrop (AUS)

Each competitor has a number. If there isn't room for the number on their clothes, athletes write it on their skin.

DID YOU KNOW?

Competitors are allowed to change their clothes at the end of each stage.

The biggest ever triathlon event took place in Chicago, in 1987. Exactly 3,888 people started the event — but you can bet not all of them managed to finish it!

Doctors and medical teams are on hand at every stage of the competition to check the athletes' health.

IRONMEN (& WOMEN)

The triathlon was invented by US servicemen stationed in Hawaii about 25 years ago. They came up with the gruelling competition as a way of testing their fitness and called it the "Ironman Race." Kate Allen (AUT) won gold in 2004, when she overtook favourite Loretta Harrop (AUS) at the very end of the race. This photo shows her on the home straight.

Each course is different in each venue, so times cannot be compared.

DID YOU KNOW?

💀 Triathletes wear padded shorts to prevent them from getting blisters on their bottom during the cycling event!

💀 The first official triathlon competition was held in 1978.

💀 The triathlon and taekwondo were two new sports that made their debuts in the 2000 Olympics.

TEMPERATURE CHECK

If the competitors are swimming in the ocean (as they did in Sydney), they are allowed to wear wet suits — but only if the temperature is below 73°F (23°C). If the water is above this temperature, they must wear swimsuits only!

HEADSTRONG

Mental strength is just as important as physical strength is in the triathlon. As well as being incredibly fit, competitors need an iron-strong will to make themselves keep going through each of the three exhausting stages.

NICE VIEW

The Beijing National Stadium, shown here, is where most of the athletic events will take place in 2008. The building is known as the "Bird's Nest," because of its unique architecture. The Bird's Nest lights up at night and seat 91,000 spectators.

There is no such thing as a triathlon world record.

(CONTINUED)

The triathlon is reckoned to be the toughest Olympic event of them all — although decathletes might disagree!

Hamish Carter (NZ)

2

ANIMAL OLYMPIANS

Even triathletes are slowpoke swimmers when compared to fish. Humans have a top speed in the water of about 4.97 MPH (8 km/h), but most fish can swim at least three times as fast.

MEDAL CONTENDERS

New Zealand's top triathlete, Hamish Carter, was ranked number one in the world during 1999 and won the gold medal at the 2004 Athens Games. His New Zealand teammate, Bevan Docherty was right behind him, and won silver at the same Games.

THE MODERN PENTATHLON

The five events of the modern pentathlon are inspired by the legend of a courageous French soldier in the nineteenth century who was sent to deliver a message.

STORY TIME

According to the story, the soldier set off on horseback, riding as fast as he could across the rough terrain (SHOWJUMPING). After a while, he came across an enemy soldier who challenged him to a duel. The messenger drew his sword and won the duel (FENCING), but as he went to get back on his horse, he heard a gunshot. The bullet missed the messenger but killed his poor horse. Quick as a flash, he pulled out his pistol and returned fire (SHOOTING). He then had to swim across a raging river (200m FREESTYLE) before running the rest of the way (3000m) and finally delivering his message.

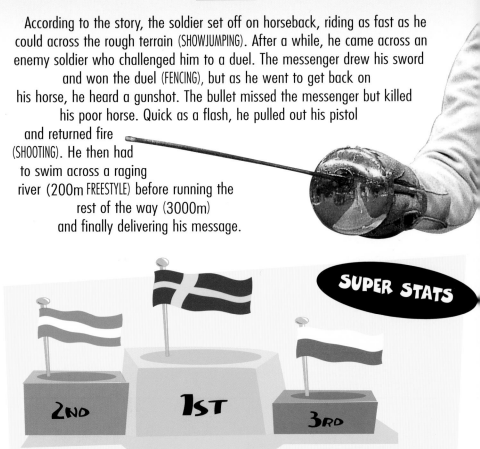

SUPER STATS

2ND   1ST   3RD

Sweden dominated the Men's individual pentathlon for more than 50 years, winning gold in this event at nine out of the 12 games between 1912 and 1968! Hungary comes in second with five golds, and Poland is third with two.

Pierre de Coubertin

MODERN BEGINNINGS

The modern pentathlon has been part of the Games since 1912. It was introduced by a Frenchman named Pierre de Coubertin. Often called "the father of the Olympics," Coubertin was also responsible for organizing the first ever Games in 1896 and was the first president of the International Olympic Committee.

ANCIENT ORIGINS

The ancient Greeks came up with the idea of combining five different events in one competition. In fact, the first ever recorded pentathlon was held at the ancient Olympic Games in 708 BCE. It included jumping, running, discus throw, javelin throw, and wrestling.

Tomas Fleissner (CZE)

DID YOU KNOW?

)) Since 1996, all five events in the modern pentathlon have been held on the same day.

)) George Patton (USA), who came fifth in the pentathlon in 1912, went on to become one of the most famous American generals of World War II — despite the fact that he did rather badly in the shooting event!

)) As well as the individual competition, there used to be a team event in the modern pentathlon. This was held for the last

---

WOMEN'S RECORDS – WORLD: No world record exists. **OLYMPIC**: Zsuzsanna Vörös (HUN) – 5,448 points.

DID YOU KNOW?

♫ At the 1936 Games, Charles Leonard (USA) scored 200 points in the shooting event — the highest possible score.

♫ Leonard's remarkable achievement was matched in 1980 by a sharp-shooting Swedish pentathlete named George Horvath.

♫ Paul Lednev (URS) won a record seven Olympic medals in the modern pentathlon between 1968 and 1980 — four in the individual competition and three in the team event.

WHAT A CHEAT!

One of the greatest ever Olympic scandals occurred during the 1976 Games when one of the Soviet pentathletes was caught cheating. Judges discovered that Boris Onischenko (URS) had tampered with the sword that he was using in the fencing event so that it registered a hit — even if he missed his opponent!

LADIES FIRST

The modern pentathlon was another Olympic event that women were first allowed to compete in at the 2000 Sydney Games. Stephanie Cook (GBR) was the first woman to win the pentathlon, taking away the gold medal at the Sydney Games.

Daniel Massala (ITA)

Graham Bookhouse (GBR)

SHOOTING STARS

In the shooting event, competitors fire shots at a target that's 10m away. Th are given just 40 seconds to fire each shot. Originally, competitors shot with rapid-fire pistol, but since 1996, they used an air pistol instead.

THE MODERN PENTATHLON
(CONTINUED)

Versatility is the key to success in the modern pentathlon as each of the events requires very different skills.

SADDLE UP

The showjumping course in the modern pentathlon is around 400m long and consists of 15 different jumps. Points are awarded to each competitor according to the time taken to complete the course. However, they lose points for knocking down any of the obstacles.

SUPER STATS

The jumps in the modern pentathlon's equestrian event are up to 51.2 inches (130 cm) high — that's taller than an average eight-year-old!

WOMEN'S RECORDS – WORLD: No world record exists. **OLYMPIC**: Zsuzsanna Vörös (HUN) – 5,448 points.

INDEX

COUNTRY ABBREVIATIONS